MODERN WEDDING SONGS

ISBN 978-1-4950-0343-1

HAL•LEONARD®
CORPORATION
7777 W. BLUEMOUND RD. P.O. BOX 13819 MILWAUKEE, WI 53213

Visit Hal Leonard Online at
www.halleonard.com

ALL OF ME

Words and Music by JOHN STEPHENS
and TOBY GAD

ARE YOU GONNA KISS ME OR NOT

Words and Music by JIM COLLINS
and DAVID LEE MURPHY

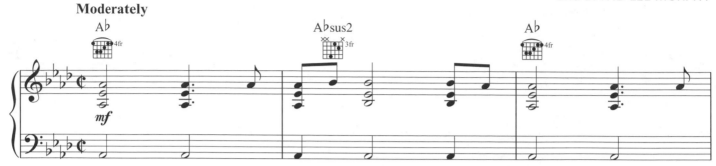

We were sit - tin' up there on your ma - ma's roof,
best ___ dang kiss that I ev - er had, ___ ex -

talk - in' 'bout ev - 'ry - thing un - der the moon. ___ With the
cept for that long ___ one af - ter that. ___ And I

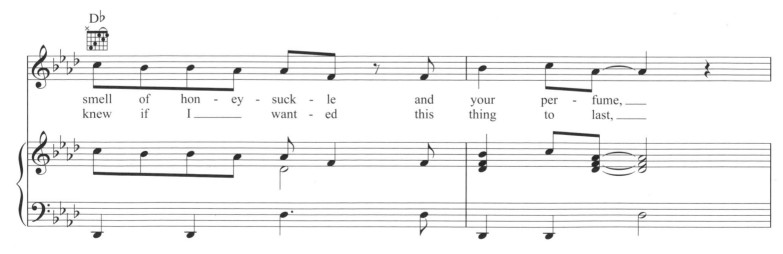

smell of hon - ey - suck - le and your per - fume, ___
knew if I want - ed this thing to last, ___

GOD GAVE ME YOU

Words and Music by
DAVE BARNES

To Coda

gave _ me you. _____

I CHOOSE YOU

Words and Music by SARA BAREILLES,
JASON BLYNN and PETE HARPER

I CAN'T WAIT
(Be My Wife)

Words and Music by JAMES BAILEY,
RYAN OGREN, JON BERRY,
PETER MUNTERS and JAMES ULRICH

* *Recorded a half step lower.*

Cmaj9   G

The Jour-ney con - cert in __ A - Z; re-

Gmaj7   Em7

mem-ber, we __ sang "Faith - ful - ly"? __ I've still got __ that old __ ho-tel __ room

Cmaj9   Am7   C   D

key.   This is the way __ I __ feel: __

% G   D/F#   Em7

I can't wait for you __ to be my wife, __ to live this life __

mf-f

I LOVE YOU THIS BIG

Words and Music by ESTHER DEAN,
RONNIE JACKSON, BRETT JAMES
and JAY SMITH

LOST IN THIS MOMENT

Words and Music by KEITH ANDERSON,
JOHN RICH and RODNEY CLAWSON

*Recorded a half step lower.

LIKE A STAR

Words and Music by
CORINNE BAILEY RAE

Just like a star a-cross _ my sky, __ just like an an-gel off _ the page, _ you have ap-
look I can't _ de - scribe. _ You make me feel I'm _ a - live. __ When ev-'ry-thing

peared to ___ my life; __ feel like I'll nev-er be ___ the same. ___ Just like a
else is ___ *au fait,* __ with-out a doubt you're on ___ my side. __ Heav-en has

song in ___ my heart, __ just like oil on ___ my ___ hands... _ Hon -
been a - way ___ too long! __ Can't find the words to write _ this ___ song. ___ Oh,

MARRY ME

Words and Music by
PAT MONAHAN

LOVE SOMEONE

Words and Music by JASON MRAZ,
BECKY GEBHARDT, CHASKA POTTER,
MAI BLOOMFIELD, MONA TAVAKOLI,
CHRIS KEUP and STEWART MYERS

THE LUCKIEST

Words and Music by
BEN FOLDS

Con sentimento

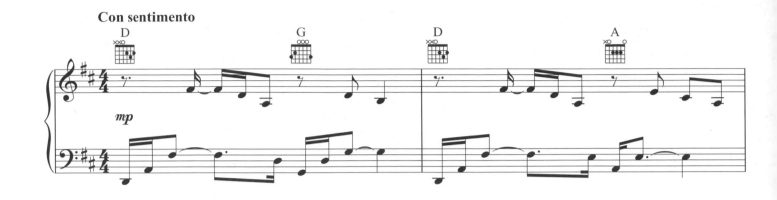

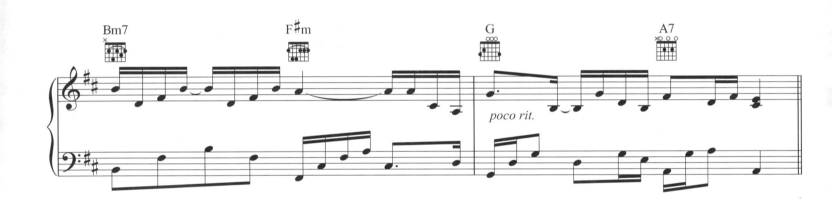

I don't get man-y things __ right __ the first __ time. _____ In

I'd been born fif-ty years __ be-fore __ you in __ a house __

door there's an old __ man who lived in-to his nine-ties and __ one day __

MAKE YOU FEEL MY LOVE

Words and Music by
BOB DYLAN

Moderately slow

When the rain ___ is blow - ing in your face ___
When the eve - ning ___ shad - ows and the stars ap - pear, ___

MARRY YOU

Words and Music by BRUNO MARS,
ARI LEVINE and PHILIP LAWRENCE

It's a beau-ti-ful night.

We're look-ing for some-thing dumb to do.

OLD FASHIONED

Words and Music by THOMAS CALLAWAY,
ALAN KASIRYE, RAEFORD GERALD
and JOE SIMON

I just smile 'cause true love does-n't go out of style. Oh, ____

(Lead vocal ad lib. on repeat)

right on time.

Ooh. ____

MY VALENTINE

Words and Music by
PAUL McCARTNEY

NEVER GONNA BE ALONE

Words and Music by ROBERT "MUTT" LANGE
and CHAD KROEGER

We're gon-na take the world _ on. _ I'll hold you till the hurt is gone. _

Ooh, ow. _ You've got-ta live ev-'ry sin-gle day like it's the

on - ly one. What if to-mor-row nev - er comes? Don't let it slip _ a - way; _ could be our

ONLY YOU CAN LOVE ME THIS WAY

Words and Music by STEVE McEWAN
and JOHN REID

you can love me _____ this way. _____

Whoa, _____ ooh. _____

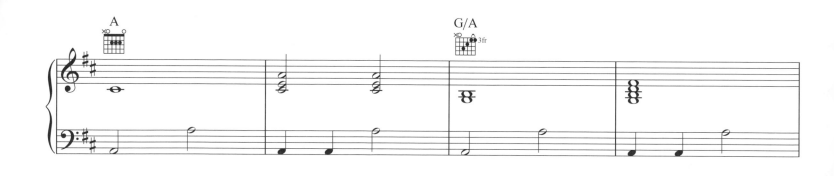

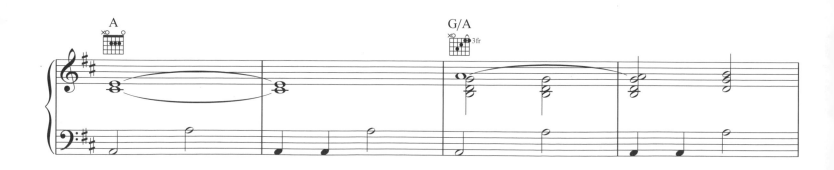

ONE DAY LIKE THIS

Words and Music by GUY GARVEY,
CRAIG POTTER, MARK POTTER,
PETE TURNER and RICHARD JUPP

Some-one tell me how I feel._____ It's

Bb/F   F   Bb/F

sil-ly wrong__ but viv-id right._____ Oh, kiss me like__ a fi-nal meal.__

F   Bb/F   C/F   Bb/F   C/F

_____ Yeah, kiss me like__ we die__ to-night._____ 'Cause,

F   Bb/F

ho-ly cow,__ I love your eyes,_____ and on-ly now__ I see the light,_____

an-y-way, __ it's look-ing like a beau-ti-ful day. ____

So,

throw those cur-tains __ wide. ____ One day like this a year __ would see me right. __

Throw those cur-tains __ wide. ____ One

THE WAY I AM

Words and Music by
INGRID MICHAELSON

*Chords implied by bass (next 20 bars).

If you ___ were fall - ing, _____ then I ___ would catch you. ___ You need ___ a light, ___ I'd find a match. ___ 'Cause I _____ (I _____

A THOUSAND YEARS

from the Summit Entertainment film THE TWILIGHT SAGA: BREAKING DAWN – PART 1

Words and Music by DAVID HODGES
and CHRISTINA PERRI

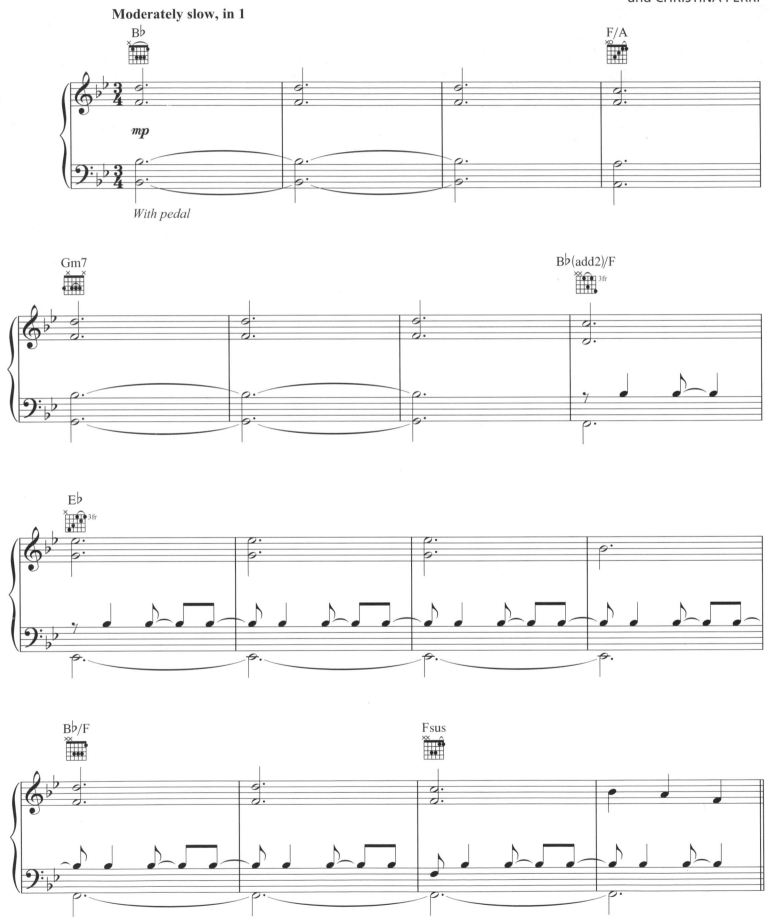

WE ARE MAN AND WIFE

Words and Music by
MICHELLE FEATHERSTONE

All the things you ___ are to me, ___

dar - ling, you have ___ set me free. ___

I'll al - ways give you ___

___ what you need ___ and what ___ you ___ de - serve. ___

WHO YOU LOVE

Words and Music by KATY PERRY
and JOHN MAYER

To Coda

D.S. al Coda

WHEN I SAY I DO

Words and Music by
MATTHEW WEST

* Recorded a half step lower.

D.S. al Coda

YOU & I

Words and Music by JOHN RYAN,
JAMIE SCOTT and JULIAN BUNETTA

Moderate Ballad

I fig-ured it out, ___ I fig-ured it out ___ from black ___ and white.
I fig-ured it out, ___ saw the mis-takes ___ of up ___ and down.

Sec-onds and hours, ___ may-be they had ___ to take ___ some time.
Meet in the mid-dle, there's al-ways room ___ for com-mon ground.

* Recorded a half step higher.

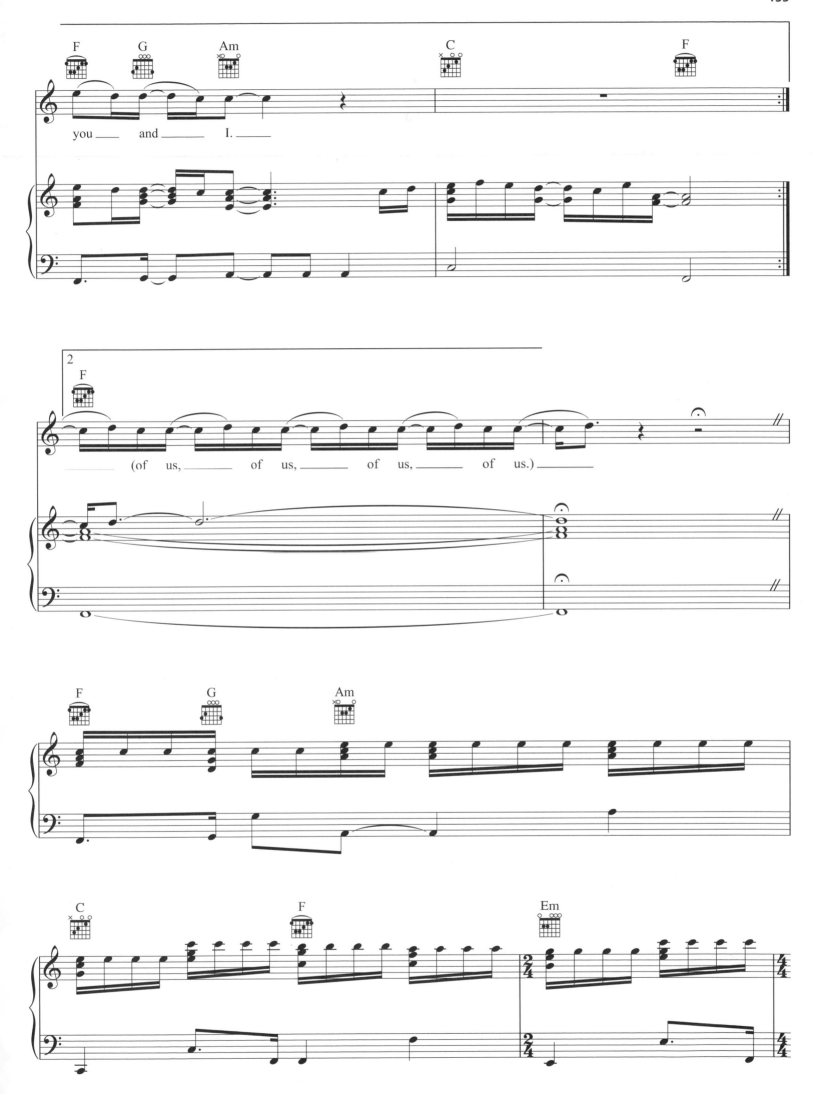

YOU AND ME

Words and Music by JASON WADE
and JUDE COLE

YOU ARE THE BEST THING

Words and Music by
RAY LAMONTAGNE

Ba - by, ___ it's been a long day, ba - by. ___

YOUR SONG

Words and Music by ELTON JOHN
and BERNIE TAUPIN

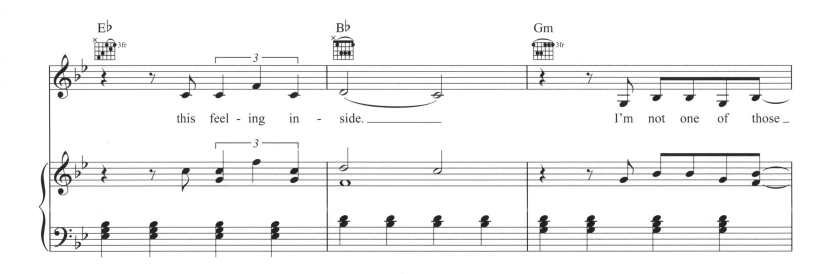

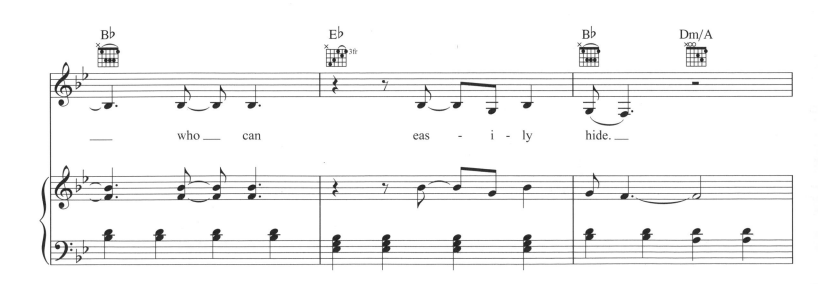

The Most Romantic Music In The World

Arranged for piano, voice, and guitar

The Best Love Songs Ever - 2nd Edition

This revised edition includes 65 romantic favorites: Always • Beautiful in My Eyes • Can You Feel the Love Tonight • Endless Love • Have I Told You Lately • Misty • Something • Through the Years • Truly • When I Fall in Love • and more.

00359198 .... $19.95

The Big Book of Love Songs - 2nd Edition

80 romantic hits in many musical styles: Always on My Mind • Cherish • Fields of Gold • I Honestly Love You • I'll Be There • Isn't It Romantic? • Lady • My Heart Will Go On • Save the Best for Last • Truly • Wonderful Tonight • and more.

00310784 .... $19.95

The Bride's Wedding Music Collection

A great collection of popular, classical and sacred songs for wedding musicians or engaged couples who are planning their service. Over 40 categorized songs, plus a website to hear audio clips! Songs include: Bless the Broken Road • Canon in D • Everything • Grow Old with Me • In My Life • Jesu, Joy of Man's Desiring • The Lord's Prayer • Marry Me • Ode to Joy • When You Say Nothing at All • and more.

00312298 .... $17.99

The Christian Wedding Songbook

37 songs of love and commitment, including: Bonded Together • Cherish the Treasure • Flesh of My Flesh • Go There with You • Household of Faith • How Beautiful • I Will Be Here • Love Will Be Our Home • Make Us One • Parent's Prayer • This Is the Day • This Very Day • and more.

00310681 .... $16.95

The Bride's Guide to Wedding Music - 2nd Edition

This great guide is a complete resource for planning wedding music. It includes a thorough article on choosing music for a wedding ceremony, and 65 songs in many different styles to satisfy lots of different tastes. The songs are grouped by categories, including preludes, processionals, recessionals, traditional sacred songs, popular songs, country songs, contemporary Christian songs, Broadway numbers, and new age piano music.

00310615 .... $19.95

Broadway Love Songs - 2nd Edition

This second edition features 47 sentimental favorites: Bells Are Ringing • Falling in Love with Love • From This Moment On • Goodnight, My Someone • Hello, Young Lovers • If I Loved You • Love Changes Everything • People Will Say We're in Love • Some Enchanted Evening • Where or When • more.

00311558 .... $15.95

Country Love Songs - 4th Edition

This edition features 34 romantic country favorites: Amazed • Breathe • Could I Have This Dance • Forever and Ever, Amen • I Need You • The Keeper of the Stars • Love Can Build a Bridge • One Boy, One Girl • Stand by Me • This Kiss • Through the Years • Valentine • You Needed Me • more.

00311528 .... $14.95

Love Songs
Budget Books Series

74 favorite love songs, including: And I Love Her • Cherish • Crazy • Endless Love • Fields of Gold • I Just Called to Say I Love You • I'll Be There • (You Make Me Feel Like) A Natural Woman • Wonderful Tonight • You Are So Beautiful • and more.

00310834 .... $12.99

Modern Love Songs

27 recent hits, including: Just a Kiss (Lady Antebellum) • Just the Way You Are (Bruno Mars) • Love Somebody (Maroon 5) • Marry Me (Train) • No One (Alicia Keys) • Ours (Taylor Swift) • Stay (Rihanna) • A Thousand Years (Christina Perri) • Unconditionally (Katy Perry) • Wanted (Hunter Hayes) • and more.

00127068 .... $17.99

New Ultimate Love and Wedding Songbook

This whopping songbook features 90 songs of devotion, including: The Anniversary Waltz • Can't Smile Without You • Could I Have This Dance • Endless Love • For All We Know • Forever and Ever, Amen • The Hawaiian Wedding Song • Here, There and Everywhere • I Only Have Eyes for You • Just the Way You Are • Longer • The Lord's Prayer • Love Me Tender • Misty • Somewhere • Sunrise, Sunset • Through the Years • Trumpet Voluntary • Your Song • and more.

00361445 .... $19.95

Romance - Boleros Favoritos

Features 48 Spanish and Latin American favorites: Aquellos Ojos Verdes • Bésame Mucho • El Reloj • Frenes • Inolvidable • La Vida Es Un Sueño • Perfidia • Siempre En Mi Corazón • Solamente Una Vez • more.

00310383 .... $16.95

Today's Hits for Weddings

Contains 25 of today's best pop and country hits that are perfect for weddings! Includes: Bless the Broken Road • Everything • Halo • I Do • Just the Way You Are • Love Story • Lucky • Marry Me • Mine • River of Love • Today Was a Fairytale • You Raise Me Up • and more.

00312316 .... $16.99

Valentine

Let your love light shine with this collection of 50 romantic favorites! Includes: Can't Help Falling and Love • Endless Love • If • Just the Way You Are • L-O-V-E • Mona Lisa • My Funny Valentine • Something • Three Coins in the Fountain • We've Only Just Begun • You Are So Beautiful • You'll Accomp'ny Me • and more!

00310977 .... $16.95

Selections from
VH1's 100 Greatest Love Songs

Nearly 100 love songs chosen for their emotion. Includes: Always on My Mind • Baby, I Love Your Way • Careless Whisper • Endless Love • How Deep Is Your Love • I Got You Babe • If You Leave Me Now • Love Me Tender • My Heart Will Go On • Unchained Melody • You're Still the One • and dozens more!

00306506 .... $27.95

HAL•LEONARD® CORPORATION
7777 W. BLUEMOUND RD. P.O. BOX 13819
MILWAUKEE, WISCONSIN 53213

www.halleonard.com

Prices, contents, and availability subject to change without notice.
Some products may not be available outside the U.S.A.

0914